John Groen

THE ROAD HOME

A journey in art and music

For Joe

THE ROAD HOME
A journey in art and music

Paintings by
DANIEL BONNELL

Songs and prayers by
GARTH HEWITT

Published in Great Britain in 2003 by
Society for Promoting Christian Knowledge
Marylebone Road
London NW1 4DU

Music transcribed and typeset by David Ball (e-mail: davidoxon@aol.com)

British Library Cataloguing-in-Publication Data
A catalogue record for this book is available
from the British Library

ISBN 0-281-05598-X

1 3 5 7 9 10 8 6 4 2

Designed and typeset by Monica Capoferri
Printed in Singapore

INTRODUCTION

When I first came across the paintings of Daniel Bonnell, I was struck by their depth, by their inspiration, by the way they reflected the hope of the gospel but also the struggle of humanity. There seemed a depth and an integrity, and although some paintings taken from the gospel can be almost polemic, wanting to point only to answers, in Daniel's paintings there is hope, but there are also shadows – there is the reality of the pain of life, and the powerful humanity of Jesus comes through as a reminder of the one who walks beside us.

I am grateful to Daniel that when I suggested I'd like to write a song around each of his paintings, he accepted this, and has always been very encouraging in the project. I find that his paintings repay time spent with them; I can see them being used in meditations and in quiet days and retreats, as a focus for thoughts and prayers in the way icons are sometimes used, and I hope the songs and the prayers add to this context, and strengthen the usefulness and the impact of the paintings, both when used by individuals or by groups.

I approached the paintings rather like a musician approaches playing in a band – in other words I didn't want to say all that the paintings were saying, I wanted to leave room for them to express themselves, and just to add some thoughts that would point to them and work alongside them. The songs rarely tell the whole story of the gospel passage to which the paintings point, but perhaps reflect some aspect of that story, and hopefully show a way in which people might respond to it, while leaving plenty of room for our own response.

There is a strength and a humility in these paintings that I believe does help us on the road home – helps us in our spiritual journey and in our own self-awareness. There is also a sensitivity and a compassion that says something to me about how we should treat others.

Thank you, Daniel, for letting me take this journey with you. I am also grateful to the Bishop of London, Richard Chartres. I have used some of his inspiring words in 'The storms of life', and he can be heard speaking them in that song on the CD.

Garth Hewitt
All Hallows on the Wall, London

the road home

On the road we look for healing
Wounded deep in mind and soul
You have walked the road before us
You alone can make us whole

We the broken-hearted people
Broken in our minds and souls
Broken in our lives and bodies
You alone can make us whole

On the road we find a welcome
On the road a touch of grace
On the road we find those outstretched arms
And we find ourselves on the road back home

May we learn to live for others
On the road that leads us home
Where we show your love and mercy
On the road that leads us home

On the road we find a welcome
On the road a touch of grace
On the road we find those outstretched arms
And we find ourselves on the road back home

Yes, we find ourselves on the road back home.

But while he was still far off, his father saw him and was
filled with compassion...

LUKE 15.20

*Thank you, God, that you walk beside us
on the road home.*

*May we take time to breathe deeply of
your love.*

*Heal our wounds, restore our souls,
refresh our dignity.*

*And as we are strengthened by your
welcome and your grace,*

may we in turn reach out to others,

*showing the love, the service and the
mercy that you have taught us.*

the road home

On the road we look for heal - ing:___
bro - ken - heart - ed peo - ple:___

woun - ded deep in mind and soul.
bro - ken in our minds and souls.

You have walked the road be - fore___
Bro - ken in our lives and bo -

us: You a - lone can make us whole. 2. We the
dies: You a - lone can make us whole.

REFRAIN

On the road we find a wel - come, on the

road a touch of grace. On the road

we find those out - stretched arms; and we find our -

selves___ on the road back home.

3. May we

3. May we learn to live for others
On the road that leads us home,
Where we show your love and mercy,
On the road that leads us home.

cast your net again

Just at the point of giving up
When the struggle had been so long
On the downward slope of despair
When everything seems so wrong
Deep waters are around us
Bitter tears begin to fall
Take the time to be silent
Take time to hear the call

Cast your net again – it's not over
You'll find hope again – it's not over
Cast your net again – it's not over
Your life is not in vain – so cast your net again

They say that the darkest hour
Is just before the dawn
But with the brand new day
Opportunities may come
You may have laboured all night
And the night has been very long
But you'll find that the darkest hour
Is just before the dawn

Cast your net again – it's not over
You'll find hope again – it's not over
Cast your net again – it's not over
Your life is not in vain – so cast your net again

[Jesus] said to them, 'Cast the net to the right side of the boat…' and … they were not able to haul it in because there were so many fish.

JOHN 21.5,6

cast your net again

VERSE

D ... **G**

Just at the point of giv-ing up, when the strug-gle had been so long, on the

A ... **D**

down-ward slope of de-spair when e-v'ry-thing seems so wrong: deep

G ... **D**

wa-ters are a-round us, bit-ter tears be-gin to fall: take the

A ... **D** REFRAIN

time to be si - lent, take time to hear the call. Cast your

G ... **D**

net a-gain: it's not o - ver. You'll find

A ... **D**

hope a-gain: it's not o - ver. Cast your

G ... **D**

net a-gain: it's not o - ver. Your life is

A ... **D** (Fine) **A** **D** *D.C.*

not in vain, so cast your net a-gain. 2. They

2. They say that the darkest hour
   Is just before the dawn,
   But with the brand new day
   Opportunities may come.
   You may have laboured all night,
   And the night has been very long,
   But you'll find that darkest hour
   Is just before the dawn.

God of darkness...as well as God of light,

wounded God...yet healing God.

When we stumble on the journey and see no hope,

may we take time to walk away from the busyness and the noise and take time to be silent.

You were not there in the earthquake nor in the wind nor in the fire but in the sheer silence;

it is there we meet you again.

May we go to the silence to restore our equilibrium –

to gain the strength to cast our net again as we realize you have not done with us yet...

there is still hope.

he broke the rules

He broke the rules when he spoke to you
To show you your value when he spoke to you
He saw deep and he saw your thirst
But love came first so he broke the rules

He broke the rules when he spoke to you
Hope broke through when he spoke to you
The disciples were amazed when he spoke to you
Because love broke through when he broke the rules

He broke rules of gender, religion and race
He showed you your dignity right to your face
A revolution started as he spoke to you
O he broke the rules and then love broke through

He broke the rules when he spoke to you
Hope broke through when he spoke to you
The disciples were amazed when he spoke to you
Because love broke through when he broke the rules

O love broke through when he broke the rules

A Samaritan woman came to draw water, and Jesus said
to her, 'Give me a drink.'

JOHN 4.7

he broke the rules

VERSE

E · E7 · A · E

He broke the rules___ when he spoke to you. To

F#m · B · E

show you your va-lue when he spoke to you. He saw

E7 · A · E

deep and he saw your thirst: but love came first so

B7 · E · %A REFRAIN · E

he broke the rules *He broke the rules___ when he spoke to*

B7 · E · E7

you. Hope broke through when he spoke to you. The di-

A · E · C#m

sci-ples were a-mazed when he spoke to you. Be-cause

2nd time D.S.

F#m · B · A · E Rpt. to end

love broke through when he broke the rules.

F#m · B · A · E · D.C.

2. He broke

2. He broke rules of gender, religion and race,
Showed you your dignity right to your face,
A revolution started as he spoke to you,
O he broke the rules and then love broke through.

*What a wonderful moment when Jesus
reached through the divisions that hold
people back.*

*Jesus affirmed the woman at the well in
a world that would not treat women
as equal;*

*he touched the 'untouchable' – reached
out to the outcast,*

*broke through the barriers of racism, of
class, of gender and of caste.*

This prophet was the great rule breaker.

*He broke the rules that bind people and
hold them back.*

*May we courageously follow this example
and exclude no one and welcome all.*

*May our churches be communities that
welcome all and may we understand the
deep joy of a gospel that nails our
prejudices and human divisions to a cross
of shame*

*and awakens us to a resurrection of
community, love, equality and joy.*

the devil's moment

When the bombers are flying in the name of peace
When people are hungry when they needn't be
It's the demon of greed when selfishness wins
It's the devil's moment

When the innocent die because our cause is right
When fear is alive and it cuts like a knife
When unfaithfulness wins and mistrust is alive
It's the devil's moment

An aeroplane against a clear blue sky
Fearfully guided by an evil eye
Both sides of the world so many will die
It's the devil's moment

Kyrie eleison, kyrie eleison
Kyrie eleison, kyrie eleison

When we turn away and pass on by
Though the cock crow we avert our eyes
When we don't speak up so the truth dies
It's the devil's moment

In Auschwitz or Palestine
Maybe on your street, maybe on mine
From Hiroshima to Rwanda genocide
It's the devil's moment

They say if a butterfly beats its wings on one side of the world
On the other side a hurricane comes
So if we say a lie on one side of the world
What will happen on the other side?

May the words of my mouth and the thoughts of my heart
Be acceptable in your eyes, O God
Or I cooperate with the darker side, and ...
It's the devil's moment

From noon on, darkness came over the whole land
until three in the afternoon.

MATTHEW 27.45

the devil's moment

VERSE
C

1. When the bom-bers are fly-ing in the name of peace, when

F2

peo - ple are hun-gry when they need - n't be, it's the

G

After v.5 to Middle section

de-mon of greed___ when self-ish-ness wins: It's the de-vil's mo -

1.2.4. | C

3.6. | C

REFRAIN
F   G

- ment.   2. When the   - ment.   Ky - ri - e - e - lei -

F/C C F G   F/C C F G

- son,   ky - ri - e - e-lei - son,   ky - ri - e e-lei -

F/C C F G   F/C (Fine) C   D.S.

- son,   ky - ri - e e-lei - son.   4. When we

MID SECTION
C   F   G

- ment.   They say if a but-ter-fly beats its wings___ on

C C/B   Am Am/G   Dm7   G

one side of the world,   on the   o - ther side___   a hur-ri-cane

C F/C C   F   G   C C/B   Am Am/G

comes.   So if we say a lie___ on one side of the world,   what will

Dm7   G   C   D.S.

hap - pen___   on the o - ther side?___   6. May the

There are choices, God – they face us all the time and each day is full of choices. We can give in to selfishness or greed or unfaithfulness

or selfish love of one's own country or creed to the detriment of others.

We can be silent when evil is happening and by our silence we tell a lie and we can allow wrong to flourish.

Or we can be inspired by your values of goodness, of purity, of justice, compassion, equality, mercy and hope.

May our choices be those that bring life rather than death –

resurrection rather than crucifixion.

May our words and our thoughts and our deeds be always acceptable in your holy eyes –

O God, our companion and our hope.

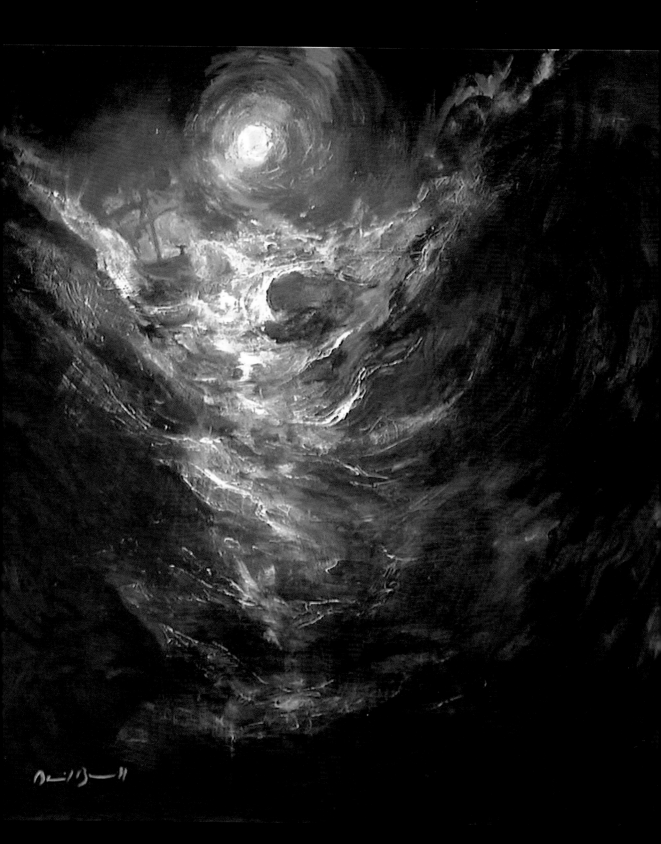

in the storms of life

In the storms of life we are not alone
In the storms of life we are not alone
Though the wind may howl and the waves may overwhelm
Even in the darkest times we are not alone

We have journeyed from out of the wastelands
We have come into the storm
It may bring perils
But it brings possibilities too
Even in the darkest times we are not alone

In the storms of life we are not alone
In the storms of life we are not alone
In the valley of despair, feeling many miles from home
Even in the darkest hour we are not alone

In the storms of life we are not alone
In the storms of life we are not alone
Though the wind may howl and the waves may overwhelm
Even in the darkest times we are not alone

[Jesus] woke up and rebuked the wind, and said to the sea,
'Peace! Be still!'

MARK 4.39

*O God, these are dark days – these are
restless times – these are fearful times –*

*Lord, hear us or we perish…yet there are
possibilities amid the perils.*

*As we sense your presence may we be
reminded of your values in the middle of
struggle.*

*May we never forget that we are not alone
– your community of love surrounds us
and you the wounded God walk beside us
in the storms.*

*Hear us as we cry to you for those caught
in the struggles for humanity, for justice,
for hope, for survival*

*– may each one have enough strength to
walk to the next day.*

in the storms of life

REFRAIN

In the storms___ of life   we are not a-lone.

In the storms___ of life   we are not a-lone.___

Though the wind___ may howl and the waves may o-ver-whelm:___

e-ven in the dark-est times   we are not a-lone.___

for the journey

You went under the water, you came up again
Ready for the journey and what it would bring
There was love all around you – the heart of God was pleased
Then you started on the journey up to Galilee

Baptism for the journey, preparation for life
Baptism of water, of glory and fire
Under the water – up for new breath
Baptism for the journey, preparation for death

On the Mountain of the Old Man the journey seems to change
Baptism of glory from the Ancient of Days
There was love all around you – the heart of God was pleased
But it's a journey to a cross where love is going to bleed

Baptism for the journey, preparation for life
Baptism of water, of glory and fire
Under the water – up for new breath
Baptism for the journey, preparation for death

The journey lies before us – there's a task to be done
When you've been through the water – a new life's begun
The journey before us may be rocky, may be steep
But there's love all around us – a love that is so deep

Baptism for the journey, preparation for life
Baptism of water, of glory and fire
Under the water – up for new breath
Baptism for the journey, preparation for death

Baptism for the journey, preparation for life

And just as he was coming up out of the water, he saw the
heavens torn apart and the Spirit descending like a dove...

MARK 1.10

for the journey

VERSE

1. You went un - der the wa - ter, you came up a - gain,
Rea - dy for the jour - ney and what it would bring. There was
love all a - round you: the heart of God was pleased. Then you
star - ted on the jour - ney up to Ga - li - lee.
Bap - ti - sm for the jour - ney, pre - pa - ra - tion for life.
Bap - ti - sm__ of wa - ter, of glo - ry and fire.
Un - der the wa - ter: up for new breath.
Bap - ti - sm for the jour - ney, pre - pa - ra - tion for death.
2. On the *Bap - ti - sm for the jour - ney, pre - pa -*
ra - tion for life.

2. On the Mountain of the Old Man the journey seems to change,
Baptism of glory from the Ancient of Days.
There was love all around you - the heart of God was pleased,
But it's a journey to a cross where love is going to bleed.

3. The journey lies before us - there's a task to be done,
When you've been through the water - a new life's begun.
The journey before us may be rocky - may be steep,
But there's love all around us - a love that is so deep.

*Jesus, you are our inspiration – your
ministry starts immersed in water then
continues immersed in glory on the road
that leads to service – on the road that
leads to the cross.*

*May those of us who have been through
the water catch a glimpse of the glory that
shows us*

*how to take the humble path – the path
of service – how to take up our cross and
follow you.*

*May we have the same love and same
spirit as you, Jesus, treating others as
better than ourselves and doing nothing
out of selfish ambition*

*but humbly looking to the interests of
others.*

*As you were obedient and knew God's
affirmation on your life*

*may we seek the road rarely travelled and
experience the awareness of the love that
is all around us.*

the shadow in the middle

I see him in a prison cell, they say he deserves to die
They see her on the street – 'we've caught her', they cry
And we all call out 'guilty', and fingers point in blame
But you're writing in the dust and you turn your face away

I see him so desperate, he's driven to despair
Nobody would listen, so he took the road to terror
And we all know he's guilty, and cry 'vengeance shall have its day'
But you're writing in the dust and you turn your face away

Who is the shadow in the middle?
Who will be the first to point the blame?
You turn and look at the shadow in the middle
I see the shadow in the middle bears my name

We always know the guilty ones, we're so quick to criticize
But who is quick to listen, and to ask the question 'why?'
Looking through another's eyes, I remember what you'd say
As I see you writing in the dust, and you turn your face away

Who is the shadow in the middle?
Who will be the first to point the blame?
You turn and look at the shadow in the middle
I see the shadow in the middle bears my name

Are you writing in the dust while you get your thinking clear?
To give yourself some time, to listen and to hear?
Can we find a way to live that cares and listens more?
Can we take the same path as you would do, Lord?

Who is the shadow in the middle?
Who will be the first to point the blame?
You turn and look at the shadow in the middle
I see the shadow in the middle bears my name

'Let anyone among you who is without sin be the first to throw
a stone at her.'

JOHN 8.7

*Serving Lord, it is too easy to be the
shadow in the middle*

*pointing the finger of blame – quick to
condemn and slow to forgive.*

*You hesitated – you did not respond
quickly – your gut instinct was not to
condemn but to restore.*

*May we see through the eyes of others –
and listen and understand and
recognize how we would have behaved
in similar circumstances and under
similar pressures.*

*As we seek to be those living right may we
never fail to empathize, to understand, to
forgive and where possible to restore*

*because this is what you have done to us
and continue to do for us.*

*Your grace and mercy is our hope – may
we pass it on to others so that the bitter
seed of self-righteousness is not allowed to
grow in us.*

the shadow in the middle

on the other side

He didn't pass by on the other side
Or turn his head or run away and hide
Or leave his neighbour by the roadside
He didn't pass by on the other side

It's so easy not to notice the victims and the weak
Or to hear the quiet voices of the forgotten and the meek
Not to reach out in love, but turn our heads and hide
But he wouldn't pass by on the other side

So don't pass by on the other side
Or turn your head or run away and hide
Or leave your neighbour by the roadside
Don't pass by on the other side

There was a world that was wounded – a world torn apart
But love for that world was so close to his heart
It was love that drove him – it was for love he died
Because he wouldn't pass by on the other side

So don't pass by on the other side
Or turn your head or run away and hide
Or leave your neighbour by the roadside
Don't pass by on the other side

He didn't pass by on the other side
Or turn his head or run away and hide
Or leave his neighbour by the roadside
He didn't pass by on the other side

And Jesus concluded, 'In your opinion, which one
of these three acted like a neighbour towards the
man attacked by the robbers?' The teacher of the
Law answered, 'The one who was kind to him.'

LUKE 10.36–7

on the other side

He did-n't pass by on the o-ther side, or turn his / your head or run a-way and hide, or leave his neigh-bour / your by the road-side: He did-n't pass by on the o-ther side. He did-n't / don't o-ther side. It's so ea-sy not to no-tice the vic-tims and the weak,___ or to hear the qui - et voi-ces of the for-got-ten and the meek.___ Not to reach out___ in love, but to turn our heads and hide: but he would not pass by on the o-ther side So don't

2. There was a world that was wounded - a world torn apart,
   But love for the world was so close to his heart.
   It was love that drove him - it was for love he died,
   Because he would not pass by on the other side.

Thank you for the example of the Good
Samaritan – when others had passed by
he stopped to help. Thank you for the
example of Jesus who did not pass by this
world but came and identified with the
forgotten and the poor, the crushed and
the broken.

To him no one was outcast – no one was
polluted – no one was to be ignored.

Jesus came to serve all equally both in
his life and in his death and he is our
example of how life should be lived.

He said 'do unto others as you would
have them do to you'.

Thank you that you stopped for us,
Lord: may we in turn stop and reach out
to others.

she gave all she had

She gave all she had – it was worth its weight in gold
It was the simple outpouring of a pure and humble soul
May our hearts be touched and our spirits be set free
To give with open hands, sacrificially

What we give in secret God sees in the light
Let our hearts be crystal-clear, not filled with pride
Let our lives be simple – may we share with those in need
Let the widow's mite be our example and our key

She gave all she had – it was worth its weight in gold
It was the simple outpouring of a pure and humble soul
May our hearts be touched and our spirits be set free
To give with open hands, sacrificially

So little means so much when the gift is everything
To give of our money, our talents and our skills
Then when our hands are emptied, they are open, Lord, to you
And we return to our homes with hearts that are full

She gave all she had – it was worth its weight in gold
It was the simple outpouring of a pure and humble soul
May our hearts be touched and our spirits be set free
To give with open hands, sacrificially

So many are oppressed – so many are poor
So what does her example mean for those with more?
Look around at God's children and ask the question 'why?'
Should some live in luxury while others thirst and die?

She gave all she had – it was worth its weight in gold
It was the simple outpouring of a pure and humble soul
May our hearts be touched and our spirits be set free
To give with open hands, sacrificially

'. . . he also saw a poor widow put in two small copper coins.'

LUKE 21.2

O God, was the widow wise to give all she
had? Did her family suffer?
Did she suffer?

Jesus certainly affirmed her giving and
she has become a model for us all because
she gave sacrificially.

Teach us to be wise givers – to be generous
givers – to be joyful givers.

For it is in giving that we receive.

If we keep our hands full we cannot
receive any more – but if we share we are
renewed.

There are huge divisions in our world
between the rich and poor;

may we be part of a community that heals
this division and allows all to be included
at the world's table –

sharing generously and thus being
regularly renewed.

she gave all she had

REFRAIN

She gave all she had - it was worth its weight in gold.___ It was the
sim-ple___ out-pour-ing of a pure and hum - ble soul.___
May our hearts___ be touched___ and our spi-rits be___ set free to
give with o - pen hands, sa-cri - fi-cial - ly.

VERSE

1. What we give___ in se-cret God sees in the light.___ Let our
hearts be cry-stal-clear,___ not filled with pride.
Let our lives___ be sim-ple - may we share with those in need.
Let the wi-dow's mite___ be our ex - am-ple and our key.

2. So little means so much when the gift is everything.
To give of our money, our talents and our skills.
Then when our hands are emptied, they are open Lord to You.
And we return to our homes with hearts that are full.

3. So many are oppressed - so many are poor,
So what does her example mean for those who have more?
Look around at God's children and ask the question 'why?'
Should some live in luxury while others thirst and die.

the warmth of love

I think I see you in the distance
I've been so cold in this place
But I see light and I feel warmth
In the eyes of a friendly face
And I breathe again and move beyond the pain
O the warmth of love brings back life again

O the warmth of love brings back life again
O the breath of life brings back hope again
The ice round my heart is melting away
As the warmth of love brings back life again

I smell the freshness of a new day
I hear birds singing, I see trees
Everything seems new, another chance to be
As I reach out and touch the earth
I raise my voice in grateful thanks
As the warmth of love brings back life again

O the warmth of love brings back life again
O the breath of life brings back hope again
The ice round my heart is melting away
As the warmth of love brings back life again

Let the warmth of love bring back life again

[Jesus] called out in a loud voice, 'Lazarus, come out!'

JOHN 11.43

the warmth of love

1. I think I see you in the di-stance, I've been so cold__ in this place, but I see light and I feel__ warmth in the eyes of a friend - ly face. And I breathe a-gain__ and move be-yond the pain; O the warmth of love brings back life__ a - gain.

O the warmth of love brings back life a - gain. O the breath of life brings back hope a - gain. The ice round my heart is mel-ting__a-way as the warmth of__love brings back

life__ a - gain. gain.

There are times, God, when we feel that
our spirit has dried up – there is no spark
and our hopes have shrunk to nothing.

May we learn to return to the reservoir of
your love and then to see through fresh
eyes with sensitivity.

Maybe the freshness of a new morning –
the deep beauty of an ancient tree –
maybe the constant movement of the sea
can spark gratefulness in our hearts.

Then hope will rise again and the chains
of negativity and bitterness fall away as
we open our eyes to new possibilities.

May we take time to look around us at
this beautiful world and to see the touch
of your hand

in friend and neighbour, in plant and
tree, in sky and sea;

and may we find the community that will
refresh us with the warmth of your love
and then...

restored to life may we reach out to others
with that same love.

LIST OF PAINTINGS

the road home: *the road home*
details: *the devil's moment*

cast your net again: *cast your net again*
details: *the prodigal and the father*

he broke the rules: *the woman at the well*
details: *judgement*

the devil's moment: *the devil's moment*
details: *the raising of Lazarus*

in the storms of life: *in the storms of life*
details: *cast your net again*

for the journey: *the baptism of Christ*
details: *the feeding of the five thousand*

the shadow in the middle: *the shadow in the middle*
details: *judgement*

on the other side: *the Good Samaritan at the door of the inn*
details: *Jairus' daughter*

she gave all she had: *the widow's mite*
details: *the widow's mite*

the warmth of love: *the raising of Lazarus*
details: *the road home*